When We
Were Young

THE 1940s

When We Were Young

THE 1940s

ARCTURUS

This edition published in 2017 by Arcturus Publishing Limited
26/27 Bickels Yard, 151–153 Bermondsey Street,
London SE1 3HA

ISBN: 978-1-78428-695-8
AD005573UK

Printed in Italy

Contents

Backs against the wall

The early years of the 1940s were a test of character for the British as Europe fell and they stood alone against Hitler. Victory in the Battle of Britain allayed fears of invasion. The nation kept calm and carried on smiling in the face of adversity. Families tightened their belts, children were evacuated to the countryside and thousands of men were sent overseas to fight the Axis forces.

Spring 1940: Fear and panic gripped Britain as the Nazis marched through Europe.

'They're not exactly the Tiller Girls!'

'Mum, I've got my pea-shooter ready just in case there's an invasion.'

'Will Daddy be back tonight, Mummy?'

'Course the Great War was much worse
than this one.'

'Dashed nuisance, neither of us knowing how to
make a cup of tea with all the servants away at war,
don't you know?'

'Mum, I'm taking my canoe over to Dunkirk to rescue some soldiers.'

'What's really touching is my wife's working in a factory
helping to make the bullets.'

Soldiers became heroes. 'Okay, if those chips are the enemy lines, imagine this pea being me.'

One man was on everybody's mind.
'Mummy, I've drawn Hitler.'

'Blimey, darling, Biffo and I pranged a few tin-cans into
the custard yesterday.'
'Sorry, dear, can you speak English?'

The Home Guard was on the alert. 'Halt! Where is the proof you're going to a school fancy dress party?'

'Just a bit worried about Christmas with the rationing; we
could become the next turkeys.'

'Angus, there's a gentleman here called Rudolf Hess. He wants to surrender to you.'

'Excuse me, ma'am, could you take your bloomers off the line? We think the Nazi bombers are using them as landmarks.'

'It's my wife asking me to pick up a nice tea service
in Paris as a bomb went off near our house and
smashed ours.'

'Never mind the woman at 36 Elm Street, Hawkins, we're looking for enemy bombers.'

'Well, he wasn't there last night.'

'Could you keep the noise down? My wife has a migraine.'

'I don't know why they all come down here every night,
but I'm glad that they leave lots of treats.'

'George? He's in the living room, Alf.'

'Flippin' 'eck, woman, forget the bloomin' fish! It's an air-raid!'

'You've got bomber-plane neck, I'm afraid,
Mrs Wainwright.'

'With all this rationing, Muriel, how do you
fancy mole pie?'

'(Sigh.) These days a red sky at night just means another
bombing raid.'

The home front

When the British population was mobilized for the war effort, the home front became a crucial battle ground. The ferocity of German bombing only strengthened the British people's will to resist Hitler. And women played a key role: dealing with rationing, recycling and cultivating food on allotments. From 1941 onwards, they were called upon to work in many unfamiliar roles.

'If the war's still going when I grow up, I'm going to join the RAF.'

'German propaganda leaflets? No, this one's: "Half-price hairdressing at Maureen's Hair Salon".'

'Last week, I was typing letters for a solicitor, now I'm shearing sheep.'

'Well, if yours is a great coat, mine's a brilliant one!'

'Typical, they miss St Paul's but hit our two-up two-down.'

'I bet the German POWs don't get treated this badly.'

'Go to sleep or the 9th Panzer Division will get you.'

'The King will be passing by this bomb site; you'd better
smarten up.'

'When I got him home and took the gas mask off, I found I'd got the wrong child.'

'Mummy keeps telling me to use more elbow grease, but
I don't know where to buy it.'

'Quick, children, that's an air-raid siren. Get under Grandma's umbrella.'

'If you ask me, our headmaster would make a good leader of the Gestapo.'

'Thanks for the sandwiches, Mum, but I think they'll have food in the countryside.'

'I'm going to call my pet rat Lord Haw-Haw, Mum.'

'Mum, look what we found in the garden.'

S.W.A.L.K. -- sealed with a loving kiss!

People began to see spies everywhere.
'If you ask me that fellow has the walk of a German.'

'I find war amazing for losing weight.'

56

'There's something about that cat that unnerves me.'

'Hey, little ladies, just think of us like the 7th Cavalry in one of those Westerns riding over the hill to rescue you...'

Glenn Miller's plane went missing over the Channel.
'Eric's gone to look for him.'

'Mum, Dad, have you been using the soap those American soldiers gave me?!'

'Corned beef, anyone?'

'(Sigh) Doesn't look like the Yanks get as far as Lower Broadbottom.'

'I don't care if Winston Churchill smokes them.'

Little went to waste.

'Tch; my husband's on his way home. He's escaped from
Colditz!'

'He's sulking cos the city lass he taught to drive the
tractor ploughs a straighter furrow than 'e does.'

'Dear Mummy, Life is much harder in the country, but
please don't worry: I am managing...'

'Dear Vera Lynn, I have often wandered over the white cliffs of Dover and never once have I seen a bluebird!'

'Have you been at the rations again?!'

'Your Dad's in the army? Hard cheese, mine's in the RAF.'

'Mummy and Daddy are in the Anderson shelter... up to no good if you ask us.'

'I'm sorry, Miss. I can't tell you why I'm late cos
Mummy says careless talk costs lives.'

'VE Day: C'mon, we can kiss loads of girls.'

'Darling, the war's over. Do you want to dance?'

Back to normal

The British emerged from World War II determined to pull together and to build a welfare state to take care of everybody, with new, improved standards in housing and health. Winston Churchill was voted out in the General Election of 1945 and Clement Attlee was given the go-ahead for reform. But Britain still had rationing, and people were forced to make do and mend for years to come.

'I'm home from the war, my wife's left me, my home's
been bombed along with the factory I used to work in.'
'We won, though, didn't we?'

Brief Encounter Part 2: 'Ow, watch where you're going with that bag. Idiot!'

'They love me, they love me not, they...'

'Five years of driving a tank never looked as scary as the state of this lawn since I got back.'

'Look at them boasting how they won the war.'

'Blooming heck!! Your snoring is louder than the Blitz.'

Money was still tight. 'Take your socks off, dear.
They need darning.'

'Mum, do I have to wear my sister's hand-me-downs?'

The Cold War began. 'Do you sell iron curtains? There's a chill wind blowing from the East.'

'(Sigh) It's great to have running water again.'

'Dashed Welfare State?!! Where's the benefit for the
likes of us?!!'

'Perhaps you should consider swapping demob suits.'

'No, son, the Americans did not win the war all on their
own; that's just Hollywood telling us they did.'

Fewer people had cars. 'Sorry, love, I keep forgetting I've got a sidecar.'

'Short back and sides? That's all I do. It's been short
back and sides for the last 20 years.'

'He says he's in the Entertainment Division, whatever that might be.'

'A steam train running at full speed, one of the finest sights you'll ever see. Let's hope we never lose it.'

'My turn now!'

'And there'll be no more wars, will there, children?'
'Oh yes, there will...'